Crikey. I'm...™

A
Grandparent

Crikey I'm... ™

A Grandparent

Contributors

Dr David Haslam
Victoria Warner
Eliza Williams

Edited by

Steve Hare

Cover Illustration by

Ian Pollock

PURPLE HOUSE

Published by Purple House Limited 1998
75 Banbury Road
Oxford OX2 6PE

© Purple House Limited 1998

Cover illustration: © Ian Pollock/The Inkshed

Crikey I'm... is a trademark of Purple House
Limited

A catalogue record for this book is available
from the British Library

ISBN 1-84118-019-X

Printed in Great Britain by
Cox and Wyman

Acknowledgements

We are grateful to everyone who helped in
the compilation of this book, particularly to
the following:

Stephen Franks of Franks and Franks (Design)

Inform Group Worldwide (Reproduction)

Dave Kent of the Kobal Collection

**National Society for the Prevention of
Cruelty to Children**

Bodleian Library, Oxford

Central Library, Oxford

British Film Institute

Liz Brown

Mark McClintock

Hannah Wren

Illustrations

Contents

Crikey, I'm A Grandparent!

The news that you are soon to become a grandparent for the first time hits most people in two distinct – but virtually simultaneous – phases.

The first is the sudden realisation that you are about to step over an invisible boundary, and all those memories of your feelings and assumptions about your own grandparents flash through your mind. 'I'm too young to be a grandparent!' is the inevitable first reaction.

The second and ultimately overpowering feeling is one of pure joy. Your child is now an adult in every sense, and you will soon be experiencing the boundless magic of seeing a new life develop and arrive in the world – but at a comfortable distance which you can at least control.

And then, if you are entirely honest, there is a third feeling which you cannot quite help smiling about. Your child, who was not so long ago (and possibly still is) a rebellious teenager who treated all your advice and words of wisdom with derision and scorn, is about to come back for your advice and help, which you are uniquely qualified to offer, and which, for once, will be valued and accepted gratefully.

The first few months after the birth of your first grandchild is a time for you to get closer to your child than you might have been since their own infancy. Your advice, cooking and knitting skills, financial aid, and just plain help around the house for a week or two will be quite invaluable for the new parents.

No one except an experienced parent has any realistic conception of just how much washing is generated by a new baby; how much clothing and equipment needs to be acquired, and then carried round on every journey, however short; and just how exhausting and, frankly, frightening, the first few weeks can be.

The loving grandparent can ease all these fears and lighten the load. The wise grandparent will do all this while taking considerable care to ensure that the husband is not crowded out of the equation altogether.

A little further down the line comes the chance to make the most valuable contribution of all: to take the baby off the couple's hands for an hour or two, at first, and then for the occasional day or weekend – to give your child and their partner a chance to spend a little time together alone, and remind themselves what life was once like, before your first grandchild arrived to change their lives for ever.

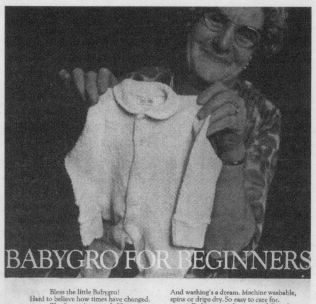

BABYGRO FOR BEGINNERS

Bless the little Babygro!
Hard to believe how times have changed.

The first suit remotely like a
Babygro was worn by Winston Churchill.

But our siren-suit actually grows as
the baby grows.

Aren't modern mothers lucky!
Our suit's in patented stretch cotton/'Bri-
Nylon' fabric.

It's got seamless shoulders which
can't rub.

We patented that too. And the
special 'Gro-Toe' foot that leaves plenty
of room without cramping the 'ten
little piggies'.

Poppers slip off and on
before your 'cuppa' has time to
get cold.

And washing's a dream. Machine washable,
spins or drips dry. So easy to care for.

Fashions may have come full circle,
but there's never been anything quite
like Babygro.

In 3 sizes right up to 2 years and
lots of colours. Babygros start at 95p
and with the first size there's a two-way
mitten cuff.

It won't be the first time you've
changed a nappy, but it will be the easiest.

You see, we gave birth to the bright
idea, since when every mother's been
expecting Babygro.

Babygro
And nothing
but the real Babygro

Babygro suits are covered by one or more of the
following GB patent nos. 931082, 930787, 1181117.
Patents pending. 'Babygro' and 'Gro' are
registered trademarks. 'Bri-NYLON' is a
registered trademark of ICI.

Babygro Limited.
16 Berkeley Street London W1X 6AP Telephone May 581

Babygro remind grandparents of the essentials in 1972.

4

Grand Days

You've become a grandparent. This may be something that you have been waiting for, and looking forward to for a long time and it is very exciting. It is a wonderful time – a new life is born, giving you a different role to play and bringing a new challenge to your life. It may also be a time when your friends will tease you about getting old, sitting in your rocking chair and taking things easy. Perhaps you are secretly unnerved by this yourself, as you have been forced to enter a new generation. Maybe you are scared you will slowly evolve into the grandparents from *The Waltons* – cranky, old, and spending your days furiously baking and mending!

78% of children surveyed by the NSPCC in 1997 said grandparents were key figures in their lives.

Yet these are hardly your twilight years. Although it is most common to become a grandparent in your fifties, this role has one of the widest age ranges possible – you could be anything from 30 to 80 and therefore, as a grandparent, there is no fixed way of living your life. You might be working, or you might have retired and have more time to help out the new family; you may be living around the corner from them or they could be on the other side of the world; you might even be caring for the child yourself.

One thing that binds you all across this diversity,

> **'My grandmother is over 80 and still doesn't need glasses. Drinks right out of the bottle.'**
>
> Henry Youngman

though, is that you have all become grandparents, a status which offers the opportunity to become involved with a new child and help out the new parents. It is a role with a rich history and worth considering in greater depth.

Grandparenting the Modern Way

So today's grandparents are a mixed bunch. Your children are also likely to be varied in age, wealth, and status and might have very different approaches to childcare from yours. There may be tension in the family – many more children are born out of wedlock and lone parents headed 21 per cent of households with dependent children in the UK in 1996, a proportion which has almost trebled since 1971. These situations have individual problems where grandparents can, and are often expected to be, a great help. This is now recognised in

> ### The Bottom Line
>
> Pampers disposable nappies were invented by a grandfather who spent the afternoon looking after his grandchild and was unimpressed with the nappies of the time. They first became available in 1961 in the US.

The grandma with a mission in Roald Dahl's *The Witches* (illustration by Quentin Blake).

the community and grandparents have their own helplines offering support with the particular difficulties that arise from divorce or step-families.

It is now clearly understood that there is a special relationship existing between a grandparent and grandchild. Whether it is due to the age gap, or because grandparents are less responsible for teaching and disciplining the child, it is clear that there can be a very deep bond between the two. This relationship has been recognised amongst counselling groups both in Britain and abroad, where grandparents are brought into contact with difficult children.

> **Only 3% of children live with extended family.**
> (NSPCC, 1997)

Research has shown that the generation gap, even though those involved are not related, brings very positive results to the children's problems.

The unique relationship between grandparents and grandchildren can also be seen in modern culture – Roald Dahl often featured a grandparent as a caregiver. In *The Witches* the grandmother saved the day!

Grandparenting in the Past

The grandparent up to 100 years ago was quite unlike today's. For a start, the chances of living long enough to see your grandchildren growing up, or even being born, were slim. Even at the beginning of the twentieth century, only five per cent of Europe's population were eligible for the newly available pension as the rest did not survive long enough to enjoy their retirement. Nowadays, however, 25 per cent of the population of Europe is of pensionable age, and in the year 2025, it is estimated that over a third of the population in Britain will be over 60. Today, living to a ripe old age is no longer a rare occurrence, but the idea of the grandparent being fit and active enough to support the new parents and look after the children is still quite novel.

It is a common misconception that the nuclear family is a product of the modern world, for it has actually existed throughout history. In centuries past, grandparents would probably only continue to live with their children once they had married if they belonged to a wealthy family with a large amount of property and land. It was also common for only the first-born male who was to inherit the property to remain in the home with

> ### Granny Smith
>
> **A crisp green eating apple from Australia, which was named after its first cultivator, Maria Ann Smith of New South Wales who, one imagines, was advanced in years, or a grandmother herself.**

> **'If I had known how wonderful it would be to have grandchildren, I'd have had them first.'**
>
> Lois Wyse

The diversity of a grandma, Part 1: Footballing Granny!

his family – any other children would usually leave once they had married. This situation is likely to have led to the image of elderly parents as domineering (figures like, for instance, King Lear), as the father would remain head of the household until he died, when the eldest son would take over. For poorer families, with less property, the fate of the elderly was not so good. It was unlikely that their children would be able to support them and they would not be expected to, regardless of English law which said they should be responsible for 'every poor, old, blind, lame and impotent person'. They would often become destitute (there were few institutions for the elderly) or live in the households of strangers and pay for their board by doing menial tasks.

In some African tribes, grandparents are given the title of *'umufasani'* or 'noble one'.

After the arrival of the industrial age (at the end of the eighteenth century), owing to the shift of families away from the countryside and into the cities and factories, things began to change. In contrast to previous times, it was the poorer families who began to live together in order to pool resources. People began to marry younger and have lots of children so that households had more hands on deck. Grandparents often taught their grandchildren the family traditions as well as essential basic skills such as cooking, mending, and building. At this time, whole families had to

11

Love at a later stage in life – hopeful contestants on *Blind Date*.

pull together, as one wage packet was not enough to support everyone. The richer families, however, now tended to live in nuclear groups and in these cases it was rare for grandparents to live with their grandchildren.

The advance of technology created even more changes for families. Industry tended to bring families together and it was common to work in family groups, even in factories. Technology changed this in two ways, as healthcare improved and many industrial practices became less arduous and dangerous: firstly people began to live longer, so it became more common to have the opportunity to have a relationship with grandchildren. However, the same technological advances also split families up, and it became more common to move and work away from the birthplace and the parental home.

Long-Distance Love

Families are living further apart – a report by the Family Policy Studies Centre (1998) shows that the number of middle-class workers with children who live more than an hour's journey away from their parents has risen by 12% since the mid eighties.

Back To The Present

Although much has changed over the last two hundred years, for most families many grandparenting traditions have remained the same, even if you are further apart and see each other less often. The role of the grandparent as the one to impart knowledge from the past generally, and also from personal family history, is still important today. You will have appropriate props as well: all the stuff that has cluttered up your attics and cupboards over the years (which you were sure would be useful one day) can be a source of fascination for a child, and a useful resource for school projects, especially in today's world, where so much has changed so quickly.

> 'The good news is that grandchildren keep you young. The bad news is that after you spend time with them you feel your age.'
>
> Joan Holleman and Audrey Sherins

Grandparents also continue the oral tradition of story-telling, talking about their own lives and the past, as well as making up stories; and they are able to conjure up magical worlds for children that seem vastly different from their own.

Modern grandparents still have much to offer the parents – you have done it all before and may be very knowledgeable about birthing and child care methods. You have the patience and experience to be actively involved and a calming influence for the parents, as well as having more time to spend with the child. Much has changed in parenting and gender roles in the last 50 years and this could be the first time that a grandfather has had time to spend with young children, if he was busy building his career when his own were growing up. Grandparents are often in a better financial and emotional position, and have the opportunity to enjoy the 'good' aspects of a child growing up, to play with them and teach them about their family and the world.

The Language of Grandparents

'All my eye and my grandmother': a Victorian Londoner's expression, which, like the alternative, 'and so's your grandmother', is a general expression of disbelief.

'To shoot one's grandmother': a mid-Victorian expression, meaning, as one would hope, to be mistaken or disappointed.

'This beats my grandmother!': this is quite astonishing.

'To teach your grandmother to suck eggs': to advise someone more experienced than you in their particular specialism. A common expression from the seventeenth century on. An earlier version, 'to teach one's grandame to spin' exists.

'To have your grandmother with you': colloquial expression from 1830 on, denoting that it is one's 'time of the month'.

It's Grand Elsewhere

Grandparents at Home and Abroad

In many cultures, both primitive and modern, grandparents are highly valued members of society. Often they are seen as the fount of wisdom and knowledge; and they are the individuals responsible for passing on ancient stories, history and tradition. This idea of the older generation being the holders of ancient lore is reflected in many different and diverse societies across the world; in older or more primitive societies, grandparents maintain a sense of continuity, of contact with the ancestors, in a less mobile community from which people do not move away.

> **In Thailand you are called a grandparent when any younger relative has a baby.**

Give a Little Respect

In some parts of Africa, age equals respect. In many of the villages of South Africa, the sacred fire of the community is, by tradition, guarded fiercely by the chief grandmother, who must keep it burning at all times – an ideal job for insomniacs. In Botswana, couples live with the parents of either partner, and

> **'My grandmother started walking five miles a day when she was 60. She's 97 now and we don't know where the hell she is.'**
> Ellen Degeneres

17

must obey all the house rules of the grandparents. The couple must also consult their elders before making any important decisions – unlike most western offspring, who adopt independence as soon as they can.

Japanese grandparents, traditionally, are also respected and treated with the reverence that they deserve – no galloping around the room with a small child yelling 'giddy-up' for them. Often the grandparents live with their children and grandchildren: they take a very active role as care-givers and teachers. As a badge of her elevated status, a Japanese grandmother is permitted to wear the highly significant colour of red. The attitude in China is very similar – it is a son's obligation to provide his parents with a happy and comfortable old age.

Grandmothers in Taiwan act as matchmakers for their grandchildren; and also as intermediaries between warring family members.

In traditional native American culture, grandparenthood is in no way about taking a back seat, and feeding the grandchildren sweets occasionally. In fact, a grandmother often has to play the role of the mother, father and teacher while the grandfather, and the parents themselves, work for physical survival. Grandparents are thought to be the final authority on all things agricultural, and farming matters are often co-ordinated by them.

The diversity of a grandma, Part 2: Baking Granny!

Labouring Together

One occasion on which you might have found yourself taking a back seat is during the birth of your first
grandchild – even fathers have only recently started to
be there. If one of you were present, it was probably
the grandmother; but even then, it is traditionally a
time for the parents alone. In South Africa, however,
the woman actually goes to the grandparents' house
to give birth. It is thought to be the safest place,
because all the family ancestors will be there; and the
grandmother will probably be past the menopause, so
the child won't be contaminated by 'impure' and
'harmful' menstrual blood.

In Korea, a grand-
mother actively
assists during the
birth, massaging
the mother and
offering prayers to
Samshin, the Birth

> **'We have become a grandmother.'**
> Margaret Thatcher
> reported in *The Times*, 4/3/89

Goddess. Once the baby is born she cooks a meal of
rice and seaweed soup for the new mother. A similar
ritual happens in Fiji, where a maternal grandmother
massages her daughter with coconut oil after the
birth, and makes her herbal drinks.

A Family Affair

In Jamaica, to live with an extended family is the
norm for most people. A woman doesn't normally
marry until after her partner has provided her with

Calling Grandmother Names

Grandma, originated in the nineteenth century
Grandmama
Granny
Grandmother
Granty, Grandy
Grannum, grannam: a shortened form of **grandam**
Nanny (though from the late seventeenth to nineteenth century, a 'nanny' was an expression for a prostitute, and a 'nanny-house' a brothel. The 'Mary Poppins' meaning did not appear until the middle of the nineteenth century).
Nana, Nan

Calling Grandfather Names

Grandada
Grand-dada
Grand-daddy are all terms for a grandfather used from the seventeenth century on.
Grandpa
Grandpop
Grandad
Gramps

several children and also proved that he can care for her and them. Often, then, three generations live together, and the young look after the grandparents as they become older. Women frequently give birth in the homes of their parents, who look after the child while she – younger and fitter – goes out to work. In some cultures, grandparents actually claim grandchildren as their own, often to help them in and around the home. In West Africa, any older woman of senior status can ask for a child once weaning is complete;

and in Colombia, some children are 'loaned' to their grandparents, providing labour whilst the family itself has one less mouth to feed.

The common theme throughout all these countries is that respect should be due to any and all grandparents. The Tallensi tribe of Ghana should have the final word on the subject – for them, grandparenthood is the finest achievement possible in their lifetime.

The Ten Most Popular Names for Children (1996)

1. Sophie	1. Jack
2. Jessica	2. Daniel
3. Chloe	3. Thomas
4. Emily	4. James
5. Lauren	5. Joshua
6. Rebecca	6. Matthew
7. Charlotte	7. Ryan
8. Hannah	8. Samuel
9. Amy	9. Joseph
10. Megan	10. Liam

There's No One Quite Like Grandma reached Number One in 1980.

William Powell and Tommy Ivo share an affectionate moment in *The Treasure of Lost Canyon*, 1952.

A Fit Grandparent

Dr David Haslam

What does it feel like to be a grandparent? In children's story books, grandparents are typically very elderly, often pictured grey-haired and sitting in a rocking-chair. Is that how you feel now? Whilst being a grandparent can be a wonderful and exciting stage of life, your first grandchild may have caused you to have very mixed feelings. You will have felt delight and joy at the safe arrival of the baby, coupled with a feeling that you must be even older than you realised, and that time is slipping by.

Modern grandparents, however, are very different from their predecessors of years gone by. After all, not only do many grannies go to aerobics classes – some even run them!

And grandparents aren't just one of nature's optional extras. Recent biological research has suggested that grandparents are fundamentally important to the human race. Most other species only survive long enough to breed, but our species seems designed so that we survive well past the arrival of our children's children. It seems increasingly likely that this is due to the fact that grandparents really do have something important to offer the new generation. Families offer security, passing on skills, knowledge and wisdom.

What you have to offer is entirely different from being a parent. You have a whole new job to learn.

The diversity of a grandma, Part 3: Ice-Skating Granny!

Your Changing Body

If you want to keep up with your growing grandchildren, then you need to keep fit. No matter how active you used to be when you were younger, you will need to work at it now. But it needn't be a chore: the solution is very straightforward:

- Exercise regularly – three times a week, doing a form of exercise that you enjoy.

- Keep your alcohol intake to moderate levels, ideally no more than 2 units a day for men, and 1–2 units for women.

- Eat three healthy and balanced meals a day, but remember that as you get older your metabolism slows, and you will need smaller quantities of food.

- Get adequate sleep and relaxation.

- If you still smoke, please stop now. Even if you don't care about your own health, you owe it to your grandchildren not to smoke in their presence. Babies exposed to cigarette smoke suffer a higher incidence of asthma, ear infections, and even cot death. It is never too late to stop. Get your doctor's advice.

- Playing with young children can be surprisingly tiring. Build up your stamina by offering to look after the children for progressively longer periods of time. A whole day with a young child may leave you shattered if you are no longer used to it.

- Whilst grandparents obviously don't have to go

through all the medical rigmarole of ante- or post-natal check-ups, you should still make sure that your blood pressure is checked at least once a year by your GP or practice nurse. High blood pressure becomes more common as you get older, and now that you have grandchildren to play with, it is even more important that the future isn't ruined by a heart attack or stroke – the most frequent results of uncontrolled blood pressure.

Your Changing Emotions

It is terribly tempting to take over when it comes to child care. After all, you have much more experience of parenthood than your son or daughter has. They, however, are the parents now. They should do it their way, and you should not attempt to impose your own opinions, or constantly say, 'Well, in my day we did it differently.' Biting your tongue can be extraordinarily difficult, but it is made easier if you simply respect your son or daughter's views.

Don't undermine parental authority. It is a recipe for domestic anarchy and ill-feeling. If your grandchildren have been told by their parents that they can't have something, don't say the opposite – however much you feel tempted.

Remember how unsure you felt when you were a new parent. Try to build up the confidence of your grandchildren's parents, rather than causing them to worry. Asking questions like, 'Shouldn't he be talking by now?' causes unhelpful pressure and anxiety.

Glamorous granny: Honor Blackman as Laura in *The Upper Hand* (Carlton Television).

Her name says it all: Supergran (Tyne Tees Television).

Remember that your grandchildren probably have another set of grandparents too, who may have entirely different views on child-rearing. Indeed, in these days of all-too-frequent marital breakdown, it is entirely possible for one child to have four natural grandparents, and for each of these grandparents to have remarried, creating another four step-grandparents. Family life can be very complicated. All the more reason for not trying to impose your views, but being available instead as support.

Remember that you have rights, too. If baby-sitting, or helping out in some other way, is inconvenient, say so, and don't feel guilty about it. Your children should not take you for granted. They did quite enough of that when they were young.

It's sad but true. Parents rarely live up to children's expectations. This is a time when your relationship with your own children will undergo a fundamental readjustment. And they have to learn that they can be both someone's parent and someone's child at one and the same time – just like you had to.

It is all too easy to see grandparenthood as just another sign that you are growing old. Instead, look at it as a new experience, a new chapter of your life, full of potential excitement. With the current increase in life expectancy, there is a strong chance that you will live to see your grandchildren's grandchildren.

When you become a grandparent for the first time, you have a great deal to offer; but you also have an awful lot of lessons to learn. Now that you are older, you know all those things that you wish you had known years ago, and will probably be able to relax with your grandchildren far better than you ever relaxed with your own children when they were young.

It may only seem like yesterday when you were bouncing your own baby on your knee. You will soon discover that your grandchildren appear to grow even faster than your own children ever did. You will also discover the truly great advantage of having grandchildren. You can have all the pleasure, then hand them back at the end of the day, and someone else can get them to bed. Now, that really is heaven!

David Haslam is married with two children and has been a GP for 22 years. He is a Fellow of the Royal College of General Practitioners, and has written numerous books – the most recent being Stress Free Parenting. *He also writes a column for* Practical Parenting *magazine, and frequently broadcasts on health topics.*

The joy of becoming a grandfather – BT's Easy Reach
advertisement from 1996.

What the Children Think

When children from six different countries were asked what their grandparents were 'supposed' to do in their spare time, this is what they said...

Switzerland	
Grandmother	**Grandfather**
to knit	to smoke
to have a walk	to have a walk
to cook	'super grandpa'
'super gran'	to read the paper
to do housework	to watch TV

Bulgaria	
Grandmother	**Grandfather**
to knit	to breed animals
to cook	to farm
to breed animals	to hunt/fish
to have a walk	to read the paper
to look after children	to read a book

India	
Grandmother	**Grandfather**
to have a walk	to have a walk
to cook	to play games
to look after children	to garden
to give affection	to do sport
to do housework	to look after children

Netherlands

Grandmother	Grandfather
to cook	to give affection
to knit	to watch TV
to have a walk	to have a walk
to look after children	to give presents
to take care of a pet	to hunt/fish

Czechoslovakia

Grandmother	Grandfather
to knit	to smoke
to breed animals	to drink alcohol
to cook	to read the paper
to read the paper	to read a book
to read a book	to breed animals

Guatemala

Grandmother	Grandfather
to garden	to do sport
to knit	to read a book
to cook	to read the paper
to look after children	to pray
to read a book	to have a walk

A Grand Old Legend

Grandparents: they've been around for centuries. That's not to say that all grandparents are horrendously old; rather that there are countless myths and legends associated with them. Some are pleasant, others not quite so – all are colourful, and here is just a sample selection.

Baboushka

Baboushka lived deep in a forest in Russia, a long, long time ago. She spent most of her time alone and saw few visitors. One day, in the middle of winter, three men came knocking on her door. The travellers were cold, lost and hungry, so Baboushka invited them in and fed them, building up a big fire to keep them warm. The men told Baboushka

> 'My grandfather's a little forgetful, but he likes to give me advice. One day he took me aside and left me there.'
>
> Ron Richards

that they were looking for a new-born king, but that the guiding star had been hidden from them by a snow-storm. When they had eaten and regained some strength, Baboushka showed the three men back to the road. Once at the road, the men insisted on following the star; and told the woman that it would lead them to a holy child, for whom they bore great gifts. They asked Baboushka if she would like to accompany them, but she refused, saying that she was too advanced in years to travel such distances on foot.

Back at the cottage, however, her loneliness impelled her to try and follow the three men. She packed a bundle of food, gathered some gifts for the child, and set off.

Baboushka, whose name means 'grandmother', never found the travellers, or the holy child. To this day she still travels, looking for him, and leaving gifts for all the babies she encounters on the way.

> 'Every generation revolts against its fathers and makes friends with its grandfathers.'
>
> Lewis Mumford,
> *The Brown Decades*

Amma

The Norse folk had great respect for their grandparents, particularly their grandmothers. In the Norse creation story, 'Amma' – whose name meant 'grand-mother' – was a legendary figure who gave birth to the race of Churls (and hence, quite probably, to 'churlishness'), a people who conducted business and practised trades.

Teleu

In Sumatra, Teleu is the god of earthquakes whose name means 'grandfather'. On completion of a new house, human sacrifices were made to this sacred figure; and blood was scattered around it, to draw his attention to the new building.

Edda

In Scandinavian mythology, the name 'Edda' means great-grandmother. The word 'eddas' translates as 'tales of the great-grandmother' and it is used to describe the great Scandinavian legends. In mythology, Edda was the first to have children, with her husband Ai. She gave birth to the Thralls, who were 'enthralled' to service as food producers for others.

Kemush

The name 'Kemush' means 'the Old Man of the Ancients', and Kemush was a North American god. He was commanded by Morning Star to create the world, making it flat, originally. Kemush later added

> 'Granny Bonds' were National Savings Certificates confined to the over fifties, before 1981.
> (Chambers dictionary)

Baboushka on her search for the Christ child, in *Myths and Legends*, by Geraldine McCaughrean (illustration by B. Willey).

The diversity of a grandma, Part 4: One-Gran Band!

valleys, hills, water, until finally he populated his new world. When his work was eventually done, Kemush followed the path of the sun – Shel – to the sky, and built himself a lodge in which to live with his daughter, Evening Star.

Kalwadi
'Kalwadi', in Australian mythology, is an 'Old Woman' whose other name is 'Mutjingga'. Kalwadi is traditionally associated with fertility rituals – which is rather bizarre, considering that the Kalwadi legend involves the grandmother swallowing her grandchildren (who were, fortunately, later cut alive from her womb).

The Old Woman of the Sea
For the Eskimos, the goddess of the sea is a grandmother figure often known as 'Arnakuagsak'.

'I'm fifty-three years old and six feet four. I've had three wives, five children and three grandchildren. I love good whiskey. I still don't understand women, and I don't think there is any man that does.'

John Wayne, 1960

Gohone

In the North American Iroquoian tribes, the spirit of winter is a grandfather figure called Gohone who raps the trees with his stick. In very cold frosts, his blows will be heard as the trees split.

Guatrigakwitl

Guatrigakwitl, for the Wishok tribes of Northern America, is the Old-Man-Above; the creator who made the universe and all creatures by spreading his hands out over the primordial vacuum.

Ketqskwaye

For the American Huron tribes, Ketqskwaye was, interestingly enough, the 'Grandmother Toad'.

Muriranga-Whenua

Muriranga-Whenua gave the Maori people her jaw bone, the bone of enchantment and knowledge. This was a reward to the hero of the Maori nation for tricking her into not eating her own grandchildren.

'Happiness is having a large, loving, caring, close-knit family in another city.'

George Burns

The classic 'grandfather' clock.

Sing Something Bizarre

Grandfather Songs

1. *Grandpa Didn't Like Much of Nothing*, Tim Lake, 1978
2. *Grandpa Got Run Over by a Beer Truck*, Da Yoopers, 1994
3. *Grandpa Got Worked Over by a Mobster*, Pat Godwin, 1996
4. *Grandpa's Birthday*, Peggosus, 1994
5. *Grandpa's Gonna Sue the Pants Off Of...*, Doctor Elmo, 1992
6. *Grandpa's Thunderbird*, Steam Donkeys, 1997
7. *Grandpapa Zorba's Dance*, Zorba, 1968
8. *Grandad's False Teeth*, Denim, 1996
9. *Grandad's Flannelette Nightshirt*, Judge Dread, 1980
10. *Grandaddy Cockroach*, Ace Moreland, 1993

Grandmother Songs

1. *Grandmother's Tea Leaves*, Emily Bezar, 1994
2. *Grandmother's Blues*, Michael Hill, 1996
3. *Grandma Got Run Over by a Reindeer*, Elmo and Patsy, 1992
4. *Grandma Sang Off Key*, Wanda Jackson, 1967
5. *Grandma Slid Down the Mountain*, Cathy Fink, 1984
6. *Grandma Smith Said a Curious Thing*, Killdozer, 1994
7. *Grandma Vanilla Don't Like Loud Rap...*, Professor Griff, 1991
8. *Grandma Vs. The Crusher*, Billy C. Wirtz, 1996
9. *Grandma's Killer Fruitcake*, Doctor Elmo, 1992
10. *Grandma's Toe Jam*, Jimmy McGriff, 1977

Copyright Notices